I0162047

John K Genda

It's Not

My

Business

John K Genda

© 2021

Editing by Savannah Cottrell - The Wonder Edits (www.thewonderedits.com)

Published by John K Genda Publishing
Visit http://www.johngenda.org/

Dear Reader,

So many say " life is short" but at the same time waste their short lives on what's not their business and what they have no control over. Most spend their lives controlled by others, subdued to opinions, drunk in gossip, hiding skeletons, and not knowing themselves and comparing themselves against irrelevant standards. This book will help direct readers from senseless interactions and activities. Every chapter in this book ends with a takeaway that highlights a focus point to remember.

It's Not My Business will help readers understand how to stay outside the boundaries of what's not their business in this brief journey called life. This understanding will help readers focus on how life is supposed to be and avoiding wasting their energy where it is not supposed to be.

Knowing and staying within your own boundaries and purpose gives tranquility to life's journey regardless of one's condition and life outcome.

I pray this book will help keep readers within the boundaries of life's purpose and direction.

With the love of Christ,

John K Genda

1 Thessalonians 4:11

And that ye study to be quiet, and to do your own business, and to work with your own hands, as we commanded you.

It's Not My Business

John K Genda

Table of Contents

DON'T LET WHAT PEOPLE THINK, SAY, OR DO DECIDE YOUR LIFE

"The best day of your life is the one on which you decide your life is your own. No apologies or excuses. No one to lean on, rely on, or blame. The gift is yours - it is an amazing journey - and you alone are responsible for the quality of it. This is the day your life really begins."

~ Bob Moawad

Life can be a failure and very miserable if it is contingent on what people say or think about us or what we think people are saying or thinking about us. Most successful people would have never gotten to where they are today if they had cared about what people said or thought about them. They understood that life is about doing whatever it takes to walk the path of the sunshine given by God.

God is the only one who has plans for our lives
(Jeremiah 29:11). Life should only be surrendered to God
and no one else. When it comes to God, life is never our
own. We should take our lives from the ownership of
other people and give it to God Who knows everything.
One should not let what people say or think about them
prevent them from resurgence after a miserable or
shameful circumstance.

Is it really your business what people say or think about
you? Why pay attention to those who contribute zero to
your life but make your life their business?

This is not to say that we should not seek counsel when it
comes to making serious decisions or that we should
never listen to sincere folks, for "Where no counsel is,
the people fall: but in the multitude of counsellors there
is safety" (Proverbs 11:14). Seeking counsel is quite
different from allowing unnecessary events and actions
of others to dictate our lives.

It is human nature to be instantly concerned about what
people say or think about us. We would not be telling the

truth if we tell ourselves that what people say or think about us does not affect us.

How rumors affect us and how we respond depends on the source. The source usually complicates the situation. When private information or lies about us circulate around, and we later discover that the source is from a confidant of ours or those we trusted, it truly bothers us. At that point, we have no choice but to be dauntless in withstanding the situation until we get to the point where we don't really care what was said and how it was perceived.

Not being easily offended by what others say about us is a cross in and of itself if our actions are for Christ and for the sake of the kingdom of God. We must take it and move forward, not backwards. It doesn't make sense to spend our entire lives defending what people say or think about us. It is not our business; it is theirs. God is the one who avenges everything as He pleases, not us (Romans 12:19). Even those we trust may hold negative perceptions of us. As First Lady Eleanor Roosevelt once said: "No one can make you feel inferior without your consent."

Some people do not care about what people say or think about them because they give people no permission to do so, and there are those who just love the spotlight and will give out their privacy just to be the center of attention. Why should one care what people should expect of them? It is up to each individual to determine whether the concerns of others in their lives are legitimate or illegitimate.

Several factors determine how we react to what people say or think about us. Such factors may include, but are not limited to, experience, growth, faith, belief, dignity, lifestyles, status, love, relationships, and other factors. We must die to people's perception about us, meaning we can't feel it to the point of destruction. It is dead on arrival.

Although I may not agree with certain folks on every issue, I do have great admiration for the ability of certain public figures to weather storms of criticism. On their way to mission or goal fulfillment, some people weathered the storms of criticism, opposition, slander, and gossip than most religious folks. Up to this day, not everyone agrees or disagrees with them. But guess what? They are moving on! It seems as if that is part of the secret of their success.

Are you moving on, or are you waiting for everyone to agree with you?

Their lives and careers are not predicated upon what people say or think about them. If they had cared about the criticisms, they would have never gotten to where they are today. They could have given up in times when things went wrong. They could have given up to the barrage of criticisms or insults on social media. They could have given up to the courts of public opinion. They could have given up to gossip around the nation. But they never gave up because they lived a life not based on the perception of others. They had no fear in their lives. They are public figures, their lives are open, and they never allow themselves to be destroyed by the feelings and thoughts of others. They have grown past their failures and shame. Now, shame bothers them no more.

Shame and disgrace have brought many down within the Christian community. Some Christians were too paralyzed to continue missions and ministry. Meanwhile, we can learn from King David that he had a powerful ministry of repentance after the shame and disgrace he experienced from adultery and organizing murder of an innocent man. He established a great ministry of repentance and restoration that we see in the Psalms today.

Some people are very concerned about what people think about them because they want a favorable opinion about themselves. They focus on building a perfect reputation and a good name. When something negative goes around about them, it hits them to the gut, and it is usually difficult for them to let it go. They want others to listen to them, and they want to listen to others as well. Some in this similar group react differently to what people say or think about them. It depends on what was said about them. Some will get upset in a forceful and truculent manner but will eventually get over it. Some will never get over it until it destroys them.

Being talkative and trying to defend everything is not always the best way to go. Quietness and moving on is sometimes the best thing to do. The bait to respond to everything can sometimes lead to more damage. We need to assess everything to see whether it is worth responding to or not.

If people with special interests choose a special way of living and care less about what people think about them, why should you care about what people think about you? If people have a problem with you, it is their problem and not yours.

Only God's perception about you matters. You are who God says you are. If you have received Christ and repented, that's all that matters. You are not condemned. You are a new person. If you happen to fail, be humble about it and sincerely repent, as King David did, and turn away from the sin. Don't wait until you are disgraced before you repent. Repenting from the thought level will save you a lot of problems. King David would have saved himself from adultery and murder had he repented at the thought level.

Another reason why we should not be overly concerned about what others say or think about us is that some people around us do not want to see us succeed. They want to see us stay right where we are. As long as we are all on the same level and in the same boat, many will be comfortable with us. The day one decides to take control of his life and start moving above the level of the natural is the day they will start saying what they want to say about you. Such folks are busy baiting you for a response so that you can damage yourself.

The truth is that everyone is not going to agree with your philosophy about life. No matter how hard you work or how excellent you endeavor to become, you will always have criticism or opposition. Some people are not going to like you anyway. The best you can do is to approach people in a positive manner because being mean is not going to change the situation.

Let us learn from Jesus Himself Who was always criticized up to the very end at the cross. He was being teased and provoked, even when on the cross, but He did not respond. If you are taking the cross and following Christ, you should learn not to respond to the teasing and provocation from the devil. Whether your choices are legal or moral, they will always be criticized, opposed, or challenged. In other words, people are busy searching for your misery or mistakes and not minding their own problems. No one has control over what people say or think, but one has the absolute authority to care or not to care about what they say or think. It is very important to understand the forms of influence that people around you have over your life.

The key is that as long as you are operating in the spirit of truth, you will be fine: "Howbeit when he, the Spirit of truth, is come, he will guide you into all truth: for he shall not speak of himself; but whatsoever he shall hear, that shall he speak: and he will shew you things to come" (John 16:13).

In dealing with people, there are questions we need to ask ourselves, such as, "Who are these people, anyway?" and "Do people make or break you?" We have no control over what people say or think, but we definitely have control as to how the thoughts or words of others can affect us. However, it is our right as adults or human beings to choose who to listen to or not to listen to. It is your right to ignore those who deserve to be ignored. It is your right to block or answer certain calls. It is your right to keep your business to yourself. It's your right to kick rumor mongers, gossip mongers, or tale bearers out of your life. It is your right to kick drama kings or queens out of your life.

The point is that drama will always continue, but it doesn't have to be around you or part of your life. Allow self to die, and let your real person come alive, and your life will not be based on opinions, likes, or dislikes. When self is dead, nothing will bother you because nothing bothers the dead. Let your real life start living! What other people say or think about us will not matter when self is placed on the cross (Luke 9:23).

Takeaways:

We do not choose what people say or think about us; therefore, it is not our business to worry about other people's choices. What they say and think about us does not belong to us because what they say or think about us is never our choice.

"And thine ears shall hear a word behind thee, saying, This is the way, walk ye in it, when ye turn to the right hand, and when ye turn to the left" (Isaiah 30:21).

EVERYONE HAS OPINIONS

"Most people are other people. Their thoughts are someone else's opinions, their lives a mimicry, their passions a quotation."

~ Oscar Wilde, De Profundis, *1905*

It can be very risky to pattern your life after someone's opinions. The majority of people with opinions usually rely on what others have said and run with it. People talk because they have the ability to talk. It doesn't mean that everything they are saying is worth listening to. They just want to feel important in the spotlight. It is good to weigh all kinds of opinions to ensure they are true before we follow them. We live in a society in which everyone is counseling everyone. It is always good to give your opinions to others, but they have to decide for themselves.

It is very essential to develop the quality to evaluate all the pieces of information we receive before we act on them. It can be very challenging to avoid the deception from opinion if we are in self. People fall to opinions because of wrong passions, emotions, affections, ideologies, and philosophies already within them. When our minds are made up, and we come across opinions that support our state of mind, there is agreement, not minding whether opinions are right or wrong. This mentality of being fixed upon non-Biblical philosophies or personal ideologies mixed with Biblical truth is deceptive and destructive. If people can have various opinions about Jesus Himself, what makes us think that people will not have opinion about our lives and how they expect us to live? "And there was much murmuring among the people concerning him: for some said, He is a good man: others said, Nay; but he deceiveth the people" (John 7:12).

There is nothing wrong with seeking facts that are helpful to us. It is always beneficial to seek the advice of experts or experience people's opinions in a particular area of interest before making a major decision. This is because there may be those who may say something on a talk show, a chat room, on the air, or on the job, and they may be totally wrong. You can listen to opinions, but it doesn't mean that you have to agree or disagree with what people say. Some people just want to talk and want others to listen.

Be careful with those who attempt to force opinions on others. A sincere person will always present an opinion to a grown-up adult respectfully, not forcefully. We can't force anyone to change their hearts. Who knows what is best for you more than your Creator? You will have a lot more problems than you do now if you set out to do everything that people tell you to do. Life is full of choices, and you can either make good ones or bad ones. The sad thing is that most people are followers and are sitting on the sidelines, waiting for someone to lead their lives.

Today, we are exposed to information that prior generations were unprivileged to have. Such exposure to information has enabled every individual to have some sort of opinion about every issue. Sources of information include talk shows on television, blogs on the internet, and posts on social media. We have access to different experts with different views on the same issues.

Besides opinions from experts and friends, opinions are also derived from personal experiences and feelings. Opinions are not professional views or statistical facts. Opinions are generally based on personal judgment. The main purpose of those with opinions can be to manipulate and attempt to gain followers. These opinion leaders are very skilled in scanning the market of curiosity and views. They know what people like and how they want to feel. They scan social media to see what people are passionate about and the lies they want to hear because it keeps them making money and in business.

Whether you believe it or not, the people you talk to or those around you do have some sort of opinion about the direction of your life and the answers to your problems. The limit to which you respond to such opinions can have a significant impact on your life. Those with opinions are always looking for a mind to be programmed by their opinions. Although you may know the ins and outs of your issues or your problems, you may still have a flood of opinions available to you.

Wisdom from God should humble us to choose correctly. Wisdom from God gives us wisdom in dealing with opinions. Fools have no desire to learn but depend on opinions. "A fool hath no delight in understanding, but that his heart may discover itself" (Proverbs 18:2). There is nothing we can do to change the opinions others hold as belief because we can't change their hearts. That is the work of the Holy Spirit. We must learn to pray for the deceived so that their eyes can be open.

Blindly accepting opinions without second thought or serious consideration can lead to your destruction. For example, let us assume that you are happily married and that you have been doing well all this time with your family. Suddenly, you expose yourself to rumors through a best friend of yours. Your best friend is single, and she continuously boasts about how much fun she is having being single. This friend portrays marriage as a curse. Ultimately, you give in to her opinion. You then begin to treat your spouse based on opinions you have believed. Your once-happy marriage begins to retrogress. Things get so bad that the relationship ends through divorce. You then try the single life but discover that it did not match the opinion you'd heard.

If you continue to listen to more opinions, things will continue to get more confusing. Opinions are not stable. They change all the time.

There are those whose specialty is to tell you what you can and can't do. Thousands of lives have been ruined because they fail to pursue their God-given convictions due to the fear of criticism or opposition. They believe in opinions more than faith. Opinions are not divine authorities or mandates. We Christians should base our lives on the authority of Scriptures, not public opinion.

We do not realize how wasteful it is to spend most of our time talking to people from whom we gain nothing. It is about time to weigh who we listen to and talk to along with the benefits of what we talk about. Are we talking to those who love to discuss people and not life itself? Are we left motivated after spending hours and hours talking to someone? Are we just curious about opinions without purpose and direction? These are questions we must begin to answer so that we can learn to keep ourselves out of things that have nothing to do with us.

Takeaway:

Blindly following opinions without a second thought or intense consideration can lead to one's chosen destruction.

John K Genda

THEY WANT YOU TO BE THEIR REMOTE CONTROL

*Control and manipulation are not love;
the outcome is a life of imprisonment
ultimately leading to deep-rooted
feelings of resentment.*

~ Ken Poirot

Everyone is trying to con or control someone or something; that is why they want to get into your business and stay there. They want you to become a remote in their hands, so they can change you whenever they want. They do not want you to think for yourself. The purpose of their influence over your life is for you to aspire to become who they want you to become and not who you were made to be. That is why it is very important to get out of a relationship as soon as possible when you realize that the other party feels you are their remote control or robot. Family members, friends, religious organizations, media, celebrities, cliques, and politicians can all compete to gain control of your mind and life. They want to tell you how to live your life.

In today's world, everything is remotely controlled. As remote controls are a normal part of life, control itself is gradually becoming second nature to some human beings. People are not remote controls or robots, and their rights and humanity should be respected. We are body, soul, and spirit.

People with good intentions may come into your life with the intent of ameliorating your life, only to leave you in a deplorable condition and constant retrogression. Family members, such as parents or siblings, who are control freaks are capable of making your life miserable and full of drama if you permit them to use you as their remote control. Some people will never experience peace and happiness as long as they stay around their controlling relatives. This is because they do have a plan for your life, and they seek to execute that plan, whether you like it or not. We have got to grow up spiritually so that we will not be in the state of being controlled by everyone and everything. "That we henceforth be no more children, tossed to and fro, and carried about with every

wind of doctrine, by the sleight of men, and cunning
craftiness, whereby they lie in wait to deceive"
(Ephesians 4:14). Not every family member or person in
our lives is bad. Although some may mean well, their
approach may seem controlling. In such a case, we must
know their spirit. Knowing people by their spirits is very
important. The only way this can happen is through the
Holy Spirit; He will reveal to us what God wants us to
know in dealing with people.

As parents, we are usually very protective and sometimes
very controlling without even knowing it. Even when
children grow up and become adults, we still have the
tendency to want to run their lives. The fact is that we
had eighteen years to teach them what we want to teach
them. If eighteen years is not enough, then the children
may not be the problem. The parent may need self-
analysis to see who is the real problem.

Let us assume that you are one of those parents who
think that eighteen years is not enough, so you decide
that you need forty years to keep an adult a baby... right?
In other words, such a parent would become too selfish
for not allowing someone to develop and discover life on

their own. I am not saying that a parent should not involve themselves in the lives of their young adult children. Children need a lot of help these days, and parents should be involved until they die. There are some exceptions, especially in situations where kids are disabled or have a medical condition. We should support and help them with God's love.

In dealing with children, each circumstance may be different. Some children may love to stay home a little bit until they at least complete their first degree or save some money so that they can start well on their own. Every good parent will love to see their kids start well, right? As long as people live under the roof of their parents, spend their money, and eat their food, they are obligated to abide by household rules. If it works well for you, and everyone is happy, I applaud that. It is all about peace and happiness.

My focus here is about those parents who are control freaks and want to exert full dominion over adult children who have moved out and are living on their own. Some parents are in the habit of living their second lives through their children. This is very common among daughters and mothers and among fathers and sons. Most mothers know exactly the type of man their daughter should marry. They set expectations that they themselves never met. When the children fall short to meet their expectation, their relationship changes. And when it comes to drama concerning in-laws, there are numerous real-life examples that the pages of this book could not hold.

I believe the religious arena has become a domain for control freaks. I am not going to talk much about other religions for this purpose because I do not know the inside out of what they do. I am familiar with Christianity from the inside out, and I am comfortable with discussing it. If you are a Christian like myself, do not get upset, but just accept the truth that some of our leaders have become control freaks. Accepting the truth will set you free.

As our leaders endeavor to build themselves empires and make themselves a name, they are becoming increasingly controlling. It is up to you to use common sense and decide what actions to take when your leader suddenly becomes a control fanatic. They quickly forget that their duty is to preach the message that convicts people and not to control them. Christians are humans, and their power of choice needs to be respected.

The Gospel of Jesus is a humble way. Most leaders do have a humble beginning, but, with time, they change and become excessively controlling due to increased following. Religious leaders who desire to control you will first start to establish themselves as the absolute authority and the path to salvation. After establishing themselves as an object of trust, then they will start working on your brain. They will continue to do so until you are no longer the person God wants you to become but the person they want you to be. You will get to a point where you can't think or reason. Before you do anything, you will want to reference what your pastor told you. This is where exactly they want you to be: their remote control. As you become someone else's remote control, your life is flipped from one channel to another.

It is very evident that members of some churches are controlled by their pastors or the so-called man of God. This so-called man of God deceptively uses games and gimmicks to make people think that he is the mediator between God and man.

Sometimes, the tactics of intimidation and fear are also used to put a grip on people's lives. For example, some pastors exercise absolute control over a man's household. Some church members will not even travel or take a vacation without the pastor's approval. These pastors are so focused on running households, but when the people ask questions, they are never around to answer. The pastor is seen to be above everyone and not accountable to anyone. He is considered the absolute authority; what he or she says is directly from God, and it is final. Members who are bold enough to ask common sense questions are considered disobedient to God in these situations. Questioning their games, gimmicks, and accountability is usually not received well. This form of religious control does affect the health of relationships and families. It is not Biblical. It is very important for people to understand when a church or a religious organization begins to operate like a cult. A major characteristic of a cult is brainwashing and control.

The media is one of the most powerful tools of control and manipulation. Control of the masses by the media is done through a consistent blitz of information. Through the media, people begin to believe what is shared over and over. Souls become what they see and hear over and over. The media knows that people have various and competing interests; that's why it operates by targeting audiences. For every interest group, there is a targeted message. The ungodly media even has a targeted message for Christians because they want control of the Christian audience as well. The media is made up of individuals who set themselves to control others.

There are those who get into others' lives with the sole purpose of control. They start as caring and loving. They say, "We are best friends for life." They try to form a bond by creating a boundary around their target. They get angry and upset when their targeted individual talks or associates with others because their ownership and control is threatened. They set unreasonable boundaries and try to cut off their access from others. We must do our best to help especially young people to know and break up negative and unhealthy bonding as soon as possible. A lot of young lives have been destroyed as a result of a cult or control.

Control can be very destructive in any form of relationship, whether it is between husbands and wives, siblings, parents, children, friends, religious leaders, and other kinds of leaders. I am not talking about setting godly boundaries within our lives. Boundaries that keep us closer to God are fine. Control is destructive in a relationship when the controllers are usually looking for something else other than a relationship. They are usually looking for someone in the form of a slave or a servant. There is not going to be any respect or value in this type of relationship. There will always be arguments or fear in this type of relationship, both at home and in front of people. Such a relationship will not last.

Recognizing this problem early and getting out as soon as possible would surely save you a lot of drama. You don't even need to argue or try to give reasons for breaking away from control freaks. Once controlled, subdued, and under their hegemony, control freaks are not willing to let go easily. The reason that they are unwilling to relinquish is that it is not easy to find someone whom they can brainwash and control.

Takeaways:

Avoid making others your remote control, and don't let them make you their remote control. This is fair enough. Submission should be voluntary and mutual, not forced. Love your neighbor as you would love yourself.

"Let nothing be done through strife or vainglory; but in lowliness of mind let each esteem other better than themselves" (Philippians 2:3).

OPERATING WITHIN BOUNDARIES OF CAUSE, CONCERN, AND PURPOSE

"I must live within the boundaries of what's my business, cause, and purpose in life."

~ John Genda

It can be very destructive to live our lives based on things that do not concern us, our cause, or our purpose in life. This is a major reason for many failed, mediocre, and unfulfilled purposes. We can't be everyone, everything, and everywhere without destructive consequences. We need to understand our boundaries based on divine purpose set for us and our sincere contribution to others and society.

We have no choice but to be extremely disciplined in a world of information. Making ourselves available to constant notifications and curiosity around the clock is unhealthy and life wasting. We rob ourselves of precious family or personal time. Let us think of all the time we have wasted in being curious in responding to things that have nothing to do with us and our purpose.

When we spend time on issues that do not concern a cause for others and our God-given purpose, we are stealing time from ourselves. It is good to have spiritual boundaries so that we are not abused or manipulated. In the days of Jesus, some of the disciples left Him because He had set boundaries for His followers. He could not allow people to manipulate or abuse the Word of God in dealing with Him. He gives us the daily cross so that we can have boundaries in our lives.

We live in the kingdom of God, and a kingdom has boundaries. "For the kingdom of God is not meat and drink; but righteousness, and peace, and joy in the Holy Ghost" (Romans 14:17). The life of Jesus was based on a purpose, and that purpose was the will of God. Jesus did not do what every religious leader wanted Him to do. He did not pay attention to those who mocked Him while He was on the cross.

Learn from Jesus that you are in the Kingdom of God. You can't do what everyone wants you to do. Don't feel guilty because you can't meet every demand and obligation of people. You are bound by righteousness, peace, and joy.

This does not excuse ourselves from helping others when we can. It is about decisions and responsibilities that do not involve us. We have no business wasting time on things that do not pertain to us. One of the greatest things robbing us of life today is involving ourselves in things that have nothing to do with our sincere cause.

Saying "It's not my business" doesn't mean that one doesn't care. It is not about escaping our responsibility of care and our due diligence to society or community. At the same time, we must understand that not a single human being has stopped the course of the universe. This means that every individual is limited in some way and another.

Boundaries and limitations exist within every organism, organization, community, or even within nations. The purpose of boundaries is usually to protect from destructive elements.

For the context of this book, the need for boundaries in one's life is for access control. A good example of access control would be an online banking system. The account owner is the only one who has access to the account. The account owner is the one who knows and holds the password to the account. You are the account holder through God in Jesus Christ when it comes to basic decisions in setting boundaries. God has given you His Word to do just that.

We need to establish boundaries in certain areas of our lives. In other words, people should not have full access to every issue we face in life. Certain areas in our lives should be restricted from the public. It is up to us to determine what needs to be known and what doesn't need to be known.

Some people are very inquisitive and want to know what they are not supposed to know. There should be limitations on the amount of information we give out about ourselves and our families. Some people have the disease of giving out too much information too soon when they meet new people. I was one of those people. We want the first person we meet to know whether we are married, have kids, or what we do for a living, but is it necessary?

The betrayals we see in the media are a result of people not setting boundaries in their lives. These betrayals should serve as a wake-up call to us. They are not one or two, but, instead, many. People are betraying those whom they have known and supported for years and years. Does trusting people make sense these days? That is the question we should be asking. Certain things need to be taken to God and only to God. If your guilt is going to be taken away, and if you are going to be healed, that healing will come from only God. I do not subscribe to the idea that certain things have to be told to certain people in order to be guilt free. Certain things are meant for only you and God. We have seen people trusted with information use it to damage others.

It is your responsibility to ensure that every perimeter of your relationship is protected as best as possible. Take certain things to God and pray that you are led by the spirit of God in dealing with people. If the spirit has not led you to open up certain areas of your life to people, then don't do it. Always remember that Samson was hurt by someone he loved dearly by causing him to open areas of his life reserved for God alone to a woman (Judges 16:4-31). Be wise.

Takeaway:

I must understand that operating outside the boundaries of what's not my business and concern is distracting from my own purpose, cause, and concern.

THE KNOW-IT-ALL PEOPLE

"Most people are more comfortable with old problems than with new solutions."

~ *Charles H. Brower*

The best way to deal with people who seem to know it all is to let them know it all. Such people can only be helped by learning the hard way. They seem to know every answer to your problems but not theirs. They are still stuck in their mess, and they want to go around telling people how to live their lives. They want to tell you how to keep a man, but they have never kept a man. They want to tell you how to come out of debt, but they are deeply drowned in debt. They want to tell you about fun, but they are miserable. Their judgment is usually after the fact. I don't mind correction when I am wrong. But these know-it-all people claim to know it all and are not willing to be corrected. Their wisdom is never practical, knowledgeable, or meek as the Word recommends: "Who is a wise man and endued with knowledge among you? let him shew out of a good conversation his works with meekness of wisdom" (James 3:13).

These know-it-all people will give you a headache if you don't move away from them. You can tolerate them if you have the time for that, but responding to them will absolutely make no sense. If you do respond to them, the debate will continue for life and will never end. They always have the last word to say. They will sit thinking about having the last word while you are talking. The conversation will continue and become useless. They are not medical doctors but will claim to know more about medicine. They are not engineers but will claim to know more about building structures. They won't just stop. In their minds, they know it all.

People generally talk about what they know, but this is not so with the know-it-all folks. They seem to have knowledge about every topic and about everything. They can't be corrected and do not receive input. Although they seem to know everything, their judgment is usually after the event has occurred. For example, they are the folks who say, "I knew exactly that Uncle Sam was going to do that." If they knew what was going to happen, they could have done something before the occurrence. This is how they seek fulfillment by pretending to know it all.

All they need is someone to give attention to their ignorance in claiming they know it all. They also need acceptance and approval. In dealing with them, you need to understand that you are not going to win a cash reward by trying to win an argument and that you will not be punished for losing an argument.

A major characteristic of those who seem to know it all is obduracy. They have a DNA of stubbornness. They feel important and fulfilled by being stubborn.

In working as a counselor at one point of my career, I came across very interesting stubborn people. One particular story I have concerns a very young and talented man. He was eighteen at the time, and he dropped out of school because he wouldn't listen to anyone. He had a yen for hanging around those who are always in trouble with the law. He was arrested once for possession, and his judgment for possession was probation for two years. During his probationary period, he enrolled in a GED program. Whilst in the program, he met some good mentors. He took the GED test and obtained the highest scores in each category. He was offered employment with a city agency. As a GED graduate, he was paid well. His salary was equivalent to those with a bachelor's degree. But the young man had a problem: he thought he knew it all. He had also not learned from the mistakes of others. Friends who had been in and out of jail continued to hang around him, and he tolerated their advice. They joked and talked about crime and thought it was fine. Finally, the same old friends got him in trouble. They were all arrested again and locked up. He lost his job and was back to square one. A lesson to be learned in this is deciding who stays and who goes in your life.

The know-it-all people will not learn from the experiences of others and will not listen. They are always right and will not accept the possibility that they're wrong. Maintaining a relationship with such people can be very challenging or complicated. They usually will not take the time to know people because they have a formula in their minds of what they want, anticipate, or expect. As a result, they go by the first impression of their expectation. And when they discover that what they anticipate or calculate does not add up, they quickly get out of it. This is the reason why most of us wonder why those who have everything do not seem to keep a relationship: they know it all. Their private or relationship life can be very complicated. Only a supernatural being can keep up with them. Instead of complementing their mates, they compete.

Let us learn to be quiet, listen, and understand that we don't know it all and that no one has ever known it all. We learn a lot by listening and being quiet. Just taking the time to be quiet and listening enables us to see things we would not usually see being noisy all the time. Let us be humble and accept the fact that we will never know it all. We only know a tiny portion of life.

Takeaways:

Let us be humble to admit that we do not know it all and that there is always room for improvement. Let us not be quick to jump into other people's business, assuming that we have all their answers when we don't.

"Let your speech be always with grace, seasoned with salt, that ye may know how ye ought to answer every man" (Colossians 4:6).

BEWARE OF THOSE WHO BRING GOSSIP TO YOU

"Whoever gossips to you will gossip about you."

~ Spanish Proverb

As the old people used to say: "The same dog that brings the bone also carries the bone." In other words, people who come to you talking about others are fishing for bones. The same "dog" that brings gossip to you is the same "dog" that carries gossip away from you. What they carry away from you may not be repeated verbatim. It is usually carried in their own distorted translation or version. Gossip creates a ton of problems and issues. It can tear apart friends and divide people through hatred, anger, and strife. "A froward man soweth strife: and a whisperer separateth chief friends" (Proverbs 16:28).

There are those who will bring their problems to you because they trust you, and it is your responsibility not

47

to put their business out. They do not come to you to gossip about others; they come to you to open up.

Others are famous for carrying other people's business. They will take information from other people and twist it, and by the time it gets to you, it is a different story. Gossip mongers have torn families apart and have caused much destruction. Always remember that people will bring stuff about others or themselves to you. It is not your business to share confidential information about others without their permission. The only exception would be if the confidential information is a crime. A spiritual person should have no business with gossip. To believe that gossip is Christian is deception. Gossip is troubling to the soul because it is usually made of the negative things about people. "If any man among you seem to be religious, and bridleth not his tongue, but deceiveth his own heart, this man's religion is vain" (James 1:26).

If you tolerate gossip, you will get caught up in the middle. People will go around saying you said this, or you said that. You will have no one to blame if you make yourself untrustworthy because you got involved in what is not your business. Accept your wrong and grow. There is no need to be part of a clique that is permeated by gossip in every way. The same person who brings and carries gossip to you will possibly make you the scapegoat of their problems. They will put your name where you do not want it to be.

I once had a coworker who was always complaining to me about things that I have nothing to do with and that were not pertaining to the business. This person complained about everything. The complaints included fellow coworkers, management, and about every circumstance. This person seemed to know something about each employee. Employees loved talking to this person, and they told her a lot of things in confidence. She dealt with people in a winsome manner, and it was easier for people to reveal things to her. This employee would bring stuff to coworkers and also carry rumors away from coworkers. Let me just quote how this employee would bring stuff to you: "This is a crazy place." "I hate this job." "I am going to start my own business and quit this job." "I am sick of this place." "This person is dating this person, and they are doing this or that." "People with worse performance are being promoted." "Managers are married and are dating girls on the job." "Everything is so disorganized in this place, and it is a shame."

Whenever she comes to me with that stuff, I always try to change the topic by saying: "Just forget about what other folks are doing and focus on what you are doing." "Just keep working till you get what you want and move on." "I am just here to work, and after that, I go home." She would continue to talk if I stuck around. But I also learnt a new trick how to deal with her. I began to move away from her as often as I could by saying: "Excuse me! I have to do thus and thus."

People later feel remorseful after seeing the destructive nature of gossip that emanated from them. They pause to reminisce about the destructive nature of things they have said about those they call friends, neighbors, and families. For some of you, this may sound familiar because you may or may not have a similar coworker who acts like this. The best answer to such a one would be, "It is not my business."

It is very important to take notice of those who come to you with what other people have told them in confidence. If they can break the trust of other people, it means that they cannot be trusted. They think that they are doing you a favor by saying, "It is just between you and me, and please do not tell anyone, but this person said this and that." Pause and think about it. The secret was between the person who told them and them, and now, the secret is between you and them. Only God knows how many more people this person will tell that it is between both of them only. Rumors, gossip, and slander can be very destructive as they become ubiquitous and can ruin relationships, careers, and families. Gossip will make the gossiper restless, and the one who receives it curious for more gossip. Gossip is a very dangerous spirit because it spreads like a virus. It replicates itself. When you give out little or no information about yourself, people have little or nothing to talk about.

There are those who think that the only way to promote themselves is to diminish the status, lives, and achievements of others. Busybodies dawdle all the time because they are idle and have no vision or purpose.

They find great pleasure and excitement in talking all the time, and they never stop talking. Even if there is nothing to talk about, they will find something to get involved with. Even when they are not asked to, they will tell you about their families and everything about themselves. We must also check our own talkativeness. We should not be giving out information that is not asked for. It is very important to test the credibility of your so-called friends. The only way to test their credibility is to know whether they are gossiping to you about others. When gossip is brought to you, the best thing to do is not to participate. It is not a good idea to talk about something that you don't know. You do not even need to make a comment or give a suggestion.

You do not have to be a psychologist or a counselor to notice when someone comes to you with rumors, slander, and gossip about those you know. They come to you because you know the people whom they are talking about. Receiving or accepting gossip or slander about those you know depends on your frame of mind. It is wrong! Stop them! If you are idle and have nothing to do, you will quickly accept rumors and slander and run with them.

People with the right mind frame know exactly how to respond to rumors. They will quickly let you know by saying: "I don't want to hear that." "It is not my business." "I can't give my opinion about the situation that is not even yours." "Why are you bringing the problems of others to me?"

Most people come to you with the problem of others not because they want to be part of the solution, but because they want to gossip. They think they have some bond with you and have the right to dump trash in your ears. As William Shakespeare stated through the titular character of Hamlet: "God has given you one face and you make yourselves another."

I once heard a story about a toddler and the mother's friend. When the friend visited the home, the toddler was just going around the friend, looking at her face and the back of her head as well. When the mother's friend noticed what was going on, she asked what the kid was looking for. The kid responded, "My mother said you have two faces. I am looking for the other one." Gossip affects children as well, and that is why we must be careful to stay away from gossip.

It is always good to deal with people directly if you have a problem with them. If you have a problem with people, you should let them know. For example, in most places of work, you have employees who always complain. If they have a problem, they do not usually go get the authorities involved. You need to let them know that you are on the job for business. Remember that you are not taking them home. Great caution needs to be exercised in dealing with people with a myriad of friends.

When nothing is happening for certain people, they will find someone to put in the spotlight. This is how the insecure will find an outlet by searching for someone they can place on the chopping block. They come to you asking about issues not because they care, but because they want to make an issue out of something. They will ask questions like, "Did you hear what they said?" They will make the grass look green on the other side to you. They will not tell you that there are brown spots on the other side until you get there.

Learn to let others who want to make issues that are not your business know that "It is not my business." Why let unnecessary things lower your productivity and trouble you? You have no control over social media opinions or others' opinions in general. They are simply not your business. You will have great peace and health in a life without gossip.

Takeaways:

It is very important to take notice of those who come to you with what other people have told them in confidence. If they can break the trust of other people, it means that they themselves cannot be trusted, especially when the issue does not pertain to you or a threat to society.

"To speak evil of no man, to be no brawlers, but gentle, shewing all meekness unto all men" (Titus 3:2).

KNOWING WHAT YOU HAVE AND WHAT YOU WANT

"But godliness with contentment is great gain."

~ 1 Timothy 6:6

Relinquishing what you know to be good in order to go after something that you have no clue about can be very risky. Just because you were told that the grass is greener on the other side, it does not mean it is guaranteed. This is not to say that you should never try the unknown. Faith involves seeking and living the unknown.

Not knowing what we want and what we have will cause a lot of headaches to us and those around us. In life, one has to be clear about what they want. Not being clear about what you want always leaves one in a recycling mode.

As a Christian, what I want should be what God wants. If God doesn't want it, then we should not be wanting it. In such an advanced world, our decisions are influenced by a variety of issues and circumstances. Such issues or circumstances include friendship, the media, desire, fun, the future, current trends, and much more. As a result, millions are left confused, guessing about what they want and what they really have. Men and women have abandoned good and loving relationships with the anticipation of upgrading to something better, only to find themselves in a deplorable and worse condition. Knowing the value of what you want and what you have will help remove confusion in your life and create stability.

There are numerous true stories of people who had it good but never knew what they had. Since they never knew what they had, they minimized it and abused it until they lost it. There are also numerous stories of individuals who have missed opportunity after opportunity because they did not know what they wanted in life.

For example, there was once a beautiful young lady who had so many friends. She was single, and so were all her friends. They lived the life of a party. She became emotionally attached to her fun group of friends. Everything about her became transformed to "me and my girls." Her decisions and her life were influenced by her girls. She could not date a man if he was not approved by her girls. Although all her girl friends desired to be married, she was the first one to get married. She got married to a family man who worked hard to create a future for his family. Unfortunately, this young lady did not know what she had, and she was easily enticed by her so-called girl friends. She wanted to be married and still maintain her single lifestyle. She never said no to the invitation of her friends to go out. She was more concerned about time spent with her friends than with her husband. Her marriage continued to be dominated and directed by her friends. Friends continued to feed her with poisons like, "Your husband is boring and is no fun," and "He is always working, and I think you should find a fun man." The words she received from her friends made her heart cold toward her husband, so she finally filed for divorce under irreconcilable differences. After her divorce, she immediately started living with the fun man who was introduced to her by her friends while she was married. The fun-loving man had some really good fun with her for a while. However, when she mentioned the topic of marriage, the fun-loving man quickly disappeared. Shortly afterwards, all her friends got married. She thought she and her girls were friends for life, but there was a hard lesson to be learned. She was shocked because a change had occurred. Now that she was divorced, and all her girls were married, none of her married friends asked her out or invited her to a bar or a girls' night out. Since she received no invitations from her girlfriends, she organized a girls' night out herself. She invited her married girlfriends to the girls' night out she had organized, and she received quite an awakening by the response she received from each of her friends: "Sorry, I have a family, and I am spending time with my husband." It was sad, but that is life. The beautiful young lady could have avoided much pain if she knew what she had and when to keep people out of her private life. She never understood the value of her marriage.

Another example is about a handsome young man who didn't know what he had. He was engaged to a beautiful and caring young woman. His fiancée took good care of him and did whatever was necessary to please him. Although he was engaged, he spent most of his time with his boys who were unmarried. His friends kept telling him about the beautiful and gorgeous women available out there. He listened to his friends and called off his engagement. This was a man who didn't know what he wanted in life. He preferred prostitutes over a wife because he was hanging around male prostitutes.

In dealing with relationships, one has to be very clear. While some go out looking for someone with whom to form a family, not everyone is looking for a family. Some people are just looking for fun and have broken the hearts of those who sincerely want a family.

Let us assume that a good person came into your life, but you failed to recognize this person because you see through your physical eyes, and they do not fit your physical criteria. You never seized the opportunity to recognize a good person, so you did not know his or her value. Your blessing came and left because you never knew what you had, and you continued to search. You sometimes come across people who you are physically attracted to. They have that pretty or handsome image you have seen on television that you have been searching for. They are that pretty face you have imagined. They are that educated man or woman you have dreamed of. Everything seems to match very well in the physical column, but the mental faculties are completely opposite. You quickly fall in love with this person. In your mind, you have met the perfect match. You begin to live at the height of the moment. You quickly tell your friends and loved ones that you have found the perfect one through your physical eyes. All your friends and loved ones admire this person. You all see through the physical eyes. You wasted years dating this person, and you rejected several good and family-oriented people for this person. At this point, you have been dating for a couple of years, and your age is not going backwards. You have expected this person to propose to you, but they never did. And, finally, you asked them about their intention, only to find out that this person does not plan to settle down. Your heart is broken, and you have to start all over again.

Another story involves an individual who thinks that she can talk her way out of anything. This individual had a good state job. However, she left the state job in pursuit of another position that she never researched. She took a position with less opportunities where she had to be retrained to do what she already knew how to do.

Sometimes, our kids don't know what they have. They are desperate to become independent as soon as they turn eighteen, not knowing that the devil is waiting for them with open arms. So many kids have destroyed their lives by not knowing what God wants for them.

On the whole, if we understand what God wants for us according to Scripture, we will avoid fewer headaches in whatever we do in this life. God has specific assignments for each and every one in every work of life.

Takeaway:
"Be careful for nothing; but in every thing by prayer and supplication with thanksgiving let your requests be made known unto God. And the peace of God, which passeth all understanding, shall keep your

hearts and minds through Christ Jesus" (Philippians 4:6-7).

COMPARING YOURSELF
TO OTHERS IS NOT WISE

*"For we dare not make ourselves of the
number, or compare ourselves with
some that commend themselves: but
they measuring themselves by
themselves, and comparing themselves
among themselves, are not wise."*

~ 2 Corinthians 10:12

Some people are concerned about what is going on in
other people's lives so that they can compare themselves
to them. They are constantly measuring and comparing
themselves to others in every way. They want bigger and
better versions of what others have. The process of
comparison continues and never ends. Boasting about
who they are and what they have makes them feel better
than others. Such people are usually envious of what
others have and jealous of who others are. They laugh on
the outside, but internally, they hate for no reason. They
want to get into your life and stay there for the wrong
reasons. They are constantly busy comparing their

relationships, status, possessions, and appearance, and it leads to their destruction. They are jealous and envious about the successes and possessions of others. They buy what they don't need because others have what they think they need. It is easy for such folks to fall into temptation to get what they want, and they do not mind participating in evil to do so.

Observing the lifestyles of the "Joneses," or the neighbor next door, just to keep up with them is not wise. Most of the time, it seems that people are focused on material items, like big houses and cars, and they forget about the real essence of what life is. It is very saddening to see those who absolutely have nothing but want to live a life that they can't afford. They go around walking with rolls of cash but don't even have a bank account. They drive new cars and are usually driving on an empty tank, praying, "Lord, if you get me out of this, I won't go back again." But soon after they are relieved of their challenges, they find themselves in the same position again because they want to be or look like someone else. They will spend thousands of dollars just to have shining rims on their cars, even when no one cares whether their wheels are shiny or not. They drive around to see who is staring at them. During the summer, they will have their windows down, hoping that someone will gaze upon them in admiration and awe. The reality is that people will look at them for only a few seconds and shortly forget about them.

There are those who live from paycheck to paycheck and desire to live the celebrity life they can't afford. They usually say, "I will get this or that when I get paid." These are folks who will use their whole paycheck just to buy the latest cell phone or tablet available. Sometimes, payday seems too far away for them; therefore, they will rush to put whatever they want on credit, not minding the interest rate and conditions. It depends on how bad they want it and how badly they want to impress people. Even if the interest rate is a thousand or a million dollars, they will still buy it because they are trying to keep up with the family next door. They care less. As long as people are saying, "Wow, look what she got," or "what he got." They will get deeper and deeper into debt because that is how their fantasy needs are fulfilled. They do not mind being surrounded by bills as long as everyone is admiring what they have.

There are those who grew up in poverty and have the opportunity to get out. They make a couple million dollars through sports, music, or through whatever talent they may have. With their new money, they will quickly want to keep up with celebrities way above their level. People tell them, "Oh my god! You look just like this or that celebrity." They accept the flattery, but in reality, they can't afford to throw away millions like those celebrities do, still afford the lifestyle, and still maintain their own lifestyles. They can try to be like the rich all they want, but their bank accounts are different. These folks think that they just need to have more than everyone else. They attempt to be like celebrities far above their level. They hire personal shopping assistants but quickly see their few millions drying up. They have brothers, sisters, or nieces on food stamps but refuse to help them move from generational poverty. Keeping up with other celebrities has caused regular celebrities to lose everything they had. There is no need for celebrities to lose homes, cars, and the basic things if they had just learned to be themselves and live according to their need-based level. Celebrities get so deep into debt to the point where they are forced to give up their homes and status.

We also need to remember that we are living in a capitalist society where we are judged by what we own. This is the reason why people ignorantly try to outdo each other. Some folks meet and usually talk about what they have in order to prove that they are doing better than others. In capitalism, people are usually drawn to success and money.

Common people also find themselves in similar conditions. For example, singles who have disciplined themselves before marriage are usually able to take care of all their bills without difficulty. As soon as they get married and begin to live on two incomes, their desires change. When their incomes are put together, they seem to make more money than they ever did before. Life seems good and easy in the beginning until they try to keep up with the neighbors next door. They have the potential of living on one income and saving the rest. But when they wake up and see different luxurious cars parked on their neighbor's driveway or a pool in their backyard, they also desire the same. Everything seems fun in the beginning, but when the bills begin to pile up, and they end up getting into the abyss of debt, it begins to affect their relationship. That's why the more money people make, the more their problems expand because they use others as measurements as to how they spend their money.

Most marriages and relationships are destroyed today because people stay in the lives of others through constant comparison. The game of comparison never ends, and it can become very destructive. People do not only compare their relationships, but some also dive further to compare their status, appearance, and their whole being to the point of wanting to be like someone else. The most prevalent comparison in modern relationships is that between pleasures.

One day, I was walking when I heard a young man talking on the phone to his friend: "You want to tell me that you have never been with more than one female? Well, I want you to rate them from one to five. Is your current girl the best?" This is how crazy people think. I was shocked about what I was hearing because this young man was a father of three children. He lives with his children's mother. This is the type of comparison that has destroyed a lot of relationships by misconstruing love. Don't get me wrong; I believe in challenging children. We must teach them early to avoid teenage problems.

Comparison is also prevalent among parents who want to live their dreams through their children. They want and expect their children to fulfill their failed dreams. They want to live with their children by pressuring them too much and setting unrealistic expectations for them.

Although envy is prevalent in every society or culture, it is more prevalent among the poor and economically disadvantaged. Envious people or friends may act like they are concerned about you, but their concern is very unhealthy. For example, if an envious person visits you and sees that your television set is larger than theirs, their next move would be to go out and buy a bigger TV so that they can have it in their home. They will keep visiting you to ensure that they have a bigger version of what you have so that they can belittle you.

Some people are very envious to the point that they won't even give credit to whom credit is due. An example of this would be people who are not educated but will get jealous of those who have that education. Instead of being happy for those who are educated and encouraging them, they will try to put them down by saying things like, "Education is not all that." Is it really their business? How is getting upset for what someone is anyone's business?

Envy and jealousy can become very destructive if they are left uncontrolled. Envy and jealousy can cause personal, family, and relationship problems. Envy and jealousy have had quite an impact on citizens living in luxurious countries such as the United States. As Americans, our desires quickly move from affordability and needs to luxury.

Although there is no need for people to become jealous and envious of others and compare themselves to others, skeptics and cynics will sit down and watch others gain economic success and become envious and jealous. They just need to get up and do what they are supposed to do.

It is never too late to do something new. It is always good to give your opinions to others, but they have to decide for themselves. Let us remember that it is ignorant to compare ourselves to others. We are not only what we see; we are body, soul, and spirit.

Takeaways:

Other people are not the tape or scale to measure your life. Stop comparing yourself to others. Learn to be content and seek satisfaction in what you have today. This will give you much peace and rest.

"For I say, through the grace given unto me, to every man that is among you, not to think of himself more highly than he ought to think; but to think soberly, according as God hath dealt to every man the measure of faith" (Romans 12:3).

EVERYONE HAS SKELETONS

"Who is wise? He that learns from everyone. Who is powerful? He that governs his passions. Who is rich? He that is content. Who is that? Nobody."

~ Benjamin Franklin

It is very unrealistic to assume that people are perfect and that they have no skeletons. Those who have been deceived to believe that they are without blemish have no spiritual connection. It has been proven over and over that those who pretend to be or claim to be perfect have more skeletons than those of us ordinary, flawed individuals. Unless their mess is put under a microscope and projected on a large screen, one would hardly know it. Only a hypocrite can think that he has no weakness.

God gave Benjamin Franklin a good insight of understanding that no human is wise enough, no human has learned from everyone, no human is powerful enough, no human is able to govern his passions, no human is rich enough, and no human is content enough. These are the things humans have tried to become for generations, but no human is able to achieve them.

Experience has enabled me to see the downfalls, miseries, scandals, mistakes, faults, defects, imperfections, limitations, failures, weaknesses, deficiencies, and shortcomings of others in a different light. It is fair to look at people and see how perfect they have presented themselves all along and how bad they have crushed others for their faults and imperfections. When they fall or tumble, their hidden imperfections suddenly become public. It becomes so shameful that they have no place to hide. Some of the smartest people on earth have made the dumbest mistakes, and I am one of them.

The pursuit of perfection is human, and the result of the pursuit is imperfection, which is also human, and it is very frustrating. Pursuing perfection is a journey of failures. That is what it is. As the great Apostle Paul said: "I do not understand what I do. For what I want to do I do not do, but what I hate I do. And if I do what I do not want to do, I agree that the law is good. As it is, it is no longer I myself who do it, but it is sin living in me. For I know that good itself does not dwell in me, that is, in my sinful nature. For I have the desire to do what is good, but I cannot carry it out. For I do not do the good I want to do, but the evil I do not want to do—this I keep on doing. Now if I do what I do not want to do, it is no longer I who do it, but it is sin living in me that does it" (Romans 7:15-20 NIV). Only abnormal people do not make mistakes. If you find an individual who doesn't make mistakes, let me know. I would like to see this wonder. That's why Jesus came to reach out to those who have issues because He knows everyone has them: "When Jesus heard it, he saith unto them, They that are whole have no need of the physician, but they that are sick: I came not to call the righteous, but sinners to repentance" (Mark 2:17). We will never get help if we pretend as if everything is well with us, and others are wrong. We are supposed to stay humble for life by fighting pride each time it shows up.

Normal people make mistakes, realize their faults, and move on. I really do not have a problem with those who make mistakes, but I definitely have a problem with the hypocrite who puts himself or herself above all. It is good to move as fast as you can from people who think that they have never done anything wrong. There is a common saying that people who live in glass homes do not throw stones. But the truth is that most people who live in glass homes do throw stones for the purpose of deflecting attention from themselves. Jesus Himself had to address the issue of those who trust in themselves and believe they have no skeletons. They were looking down on others. "And he spake this parable unto certain which trusted in themselves that they were righteous, and despised others" (Luke 18:9).

Hence, it comes to this issue: I see a great hypocrisy and deception with religious institutions. The problem I have with some religious folks is that they will not admit their wrong until they are exposed and humiliated.

Let me speak from a Christian's point of view. Most Christians have this perfect presentation of themselves, and when it doesn't add up, instead of coming up real, they feel embarrassed. For example, there are those Christians who think that they have no problem because their situation is financial. They see nothing wrong about being kleptomaniacs in financial institutions or on church boards. They see no problem with nepotism and corruption. When sanctimonious individuals are trained to pretend to act perfect, they do have a real problem; I mean a real big problem. There is no need to pretend to be perfect. One just needs to learn to work hard in preventing the same mistakes in life by allowing the Holy Spirit to lead them moving forward. Life is not that long to keep making the same mistakes over and over. It can be too late in the game to repeat the same mistakes.

Being a religious person does not, by default, make you trustworthy. Times have changed, and people have changed. Religious practices we read about hundred years ago are quite different from what we see and experience today. If you try to live according to the standard set by people, you will never make it. As Christians, we know it is impossible to live the divine life without the help of God. We bring our mistakes to the cross for help.

Takeaways:
Learn to deal with others with grace regardless of how worse you think the condition is.

"The self-righteous scream judgments against others to hide the noise of skeletons dancing in their own closets." - John Mark Green

YOU DON'T KNOW ME

*"No one can know a person's thoughts
except that person's own spirit, and no
one can know God's thoughts except
God's own Spirit."*

~ 1 Corinthians 2:11 NLT

It can be crazy sometimes to hear people say, "I know thus and thus," or "I knew they were going to do thus and thus." The reality is that they really do not know who you really are. If they knew who you were, they would not wait for incidences to occur before they define you. Since they could not predetermine your actions and your ways, that means they do not know you.

It is not safe to boast that you know this or that person because people are always changing. They may attempt to know you through speculation or falsity, but they really do not know you. No one knows what is in your heart, so no one on earth truly knows you. This applies to even your mate or your parents. Even your mother, who carried you for nine months, still struggles to know who you really are. Time brings change; some may change for the better, and others may change for the worse. You think you know me, but you really don't. The only One Who knows you is God, Who has the ability to see through every soul and spirit.

The human sinful nature is very dangerous and can manifest in various ways. There are numerous examples of people we never thought would do certain things who ended up doing the worst or the best. Neighbors become shocked when people they have known to be nice and kind for years and without any criminal record commit horrible crimes. Religious institutions are shocked when those considered righteous commit the most vile and despicable acts. It is very important to understand that we will never know or predict changes within people. Let us hope and always pray for people to be good.

The people you knew years ago may not necessarily be the people you know today, so stop assuming that you know them. With time, good people may become bad, and some bad people may become good. Some are blessed to remain the same way. The evil people you knew years ago may have repented and have done so better than you.

The only benefit from knowing someone's background is to identify certain behavior patterns for the purpose of making decisions. If your purpose for searching someone's background is just for curiosity, then it is not your business.

When looking at the behavior patterns of the past of others, we need to be careful so that we are not prejudiced. Some people may exhibit certain behavior patterns at some point in their lives because of youth or immaturity, but they will later change. That is why it is not always fair to judge people based on their past experiences. In some instances, it is good to exercise sound judgment.

When dealing with what you know about others, you will come across those who you think will never change because of what you think you know about them. Your paradigm about others is based on what you know or anticipate about them.

Even when people change, you continue to see them as how they were in the past, meaning you really do not know them. People change so much within a matter of a couple of years, and sometimes, people are in the midst of change. You can't predict what somebody can do this year or that year. Humans are not business trends. There are lots of things that change people, including money. The people you know from high school may not be the same today. When people leave home and go to college, they get exposed to so many things. Some are very lucky to be exposed and attracted to the right things, while others are not. Some get exposed to the wrong things, such as drugs, alcohol, and too much clubbing, and they end up becoming a different person that people no longer know. Therefore, you definitely had no idea of who your high school friends are and what they are doing. You were quite a different person the last time they remembered you and what you were doing. Also, presidents of the United States have changed positions on so many issues. We usually see and admire the talents of gifted men and women, but we don't see what goes on underneath. There is a lot more of what goes on underneath that we do not even know about.

As humans, we are all subject to deception if we are not careful. More clearly, we can't make the judgement of knowing someone because there is a lot more that could be going on that we had no idea about. Even when we look at people, we do not see things that line up with our own judgment, so we can't look at a person and know who they are and what they are going to become. Our judgment pushes people towards certain things. Just because you are good at something, that doesn't mean it is going to be your career path. For example, just because you love to talk and argue, that doesn't mean that you are going to be a lawyer. Parents of such talkative kids will usually get off track and start boasting about things that make no sense. They will say words like, "My baby is going to be a lawyer" and do not even know that there are various types of lawyers. There are lawyers who do not even talk much; they work for corporations sitting in offices and doing research.

The actions of certain individuals are kind of predictable because you have seen them live in the past over and over again. Although they continue to live their past in the present, again, you really do not know them as well as you think. People can change and have changed drastically.

This example here is just a scenario. It does not mean I support or promote divorce. Divorce happens among us, but God hates it. So, that being said, let us assume that Paul and Jane may be in their fifth marriage. Being married five times may mean that they need to learn certain things from previous relationships. But, again, who am I to know all things? I will pray and hope for their mercy. That is their business. Although something may be wrong somewhere, there are always two sides to a story. They may change, or they may not change. Who knows? It may make sense to say that you know Jane and Paul and that they are always getting married and divorced. But, again, it is not your business because you may not fully understand their situation or the sin involved. Pray for their salvation. It may be that they are the innocent ones, and they may just happen to fall trap after trap because of perpetual darkness in their lives. The Bible is very clear about divorce and remarriage, and there is no need to debate that. At the end, all we can do is to pray and hope God shows mercy: "The Lord replied, 'I will make all my goodness pass before you, and I will call out my name, Yahweh, before you. For I will show mercy to anyone I choose, and I will show compassion to anyone I choose'" (Exodus 33:19 NLT). Let the Word judge the situation because you only know what the Word says about the situation, but in reality, you still do not know them. Now, you think you really know Paul and Jane, but all you really know about them is their past, and you want to use it against them. You go around telling gossip mongers and rumor mongers that you know Paul and Jane. You gossip about them and tell people that they will never settle down because they are always in and out of relationships. Your paradigm about Paul and Jane is their past. All of a sudden, divine interruption occurred, their life changed, and you were proven to be a liar. They repented and found peace with God. I don't understand everything, but one thing I know as the last resort is to point people to God. Regardless of how bad people's sins may be, let us hope that the grace of God gives them a chance if they repent sincerely. Let it be noted that I am not a fan of divorce, and this scenario is not encouraging folks to keep divorcing. If you make a mistake, purpose not to continue. You thought you knew then that they would never change, but they did.

Let us never assume that we know people based on what we see in them or experience with them. People are always changing for the better or for the worse. We can't hold the same opinions of people based on a status we knew in the past. Let us pray that the Spirit will lead them.

Takeaway:

Never assume you know people. Try to know the spirits of the people whom you are working with.

DO YOU KNOW YOURSELF?

"For that which I do I allow not: for what I would, that do I not; but what I hate, that do I. If then I do that which I would not, I consent unto the law that it is good.

Now then it is no more I that do it, but sin that dwelleth in me."

~ Romans 7:15-17

Most people are looking for themselves because they feel they have lost themselves. They spend so much time trying to look for themselves by doing anything. The self-desire of people to know and establish themselves usually ends in dissatisfaction. All the unrest and hustle in trying to know oneself outside of God ends in disappointment and discontent. They are easily addicted by the feelings of being wanted, which puts them in the position of an insecure chameleon, always switching to fit different suits. They act impulsively and never think about the positive or negative effect of their actions on people at the moment. The moment of wanting what they desire is the most important to them. They really do not know what they need and who they are. Instead of waiting for what they need, they will take the first thing that comes along. Their choice may be the best thing for the moment, but it is actually different from what they want, and they will regret it later. Again, they are upset because what they thought they wanted is not what they got.

Although we all make mistakes, and we may make the same mistakes again, it can be very frustrating to be forty years old and repeating the same mistakes over and over. Wandering around at forty because of not knowing yourself will return you to square one. At a certain level of maturity, we should be settling for what God wants for us and not what everyone else wants. Just because everybody else has it or is doing it, that doesn't mean that it is right for us. They don't know themselves because they refuse to submit themselves to God. What God wants for us is the only place of satisfaction.

At certain times and moments in life, people think that their choices and desires are the most important thing in life. Such folks never take the time to pause and think that certain things in life are in one ear and out the other. The realization of one not knowing themselves emerges especially when they are exposed to a lot of new things. They quickly get excited and think that they need to get involved in whatever is going on. For example, when certain people get to a new city, they start acting crazy, thinking it is cool to do so. They want to impress others by false security. They usually try to do things in front of certain people. They are never fine with who they are and act differently as a result. If a certain individual walks within their space, they will start acting contrary to their own nature all of a sudden. They never pause to think how long their performance is going to last. If one can just ask themselves the question: "Is anyone really going to care about this in six months?" If your answer is definitely no, then it should not be your focus.

We have no clue of who we are due to the sinful nature of the human heart. Our own hearts are deceiving. The only help for us is to take up the cross. Peace can only be found in Christ. Christ knows us better than we know ourselves.

Takeaways:

"The heart is deceitful above all things, and desperately wicked: who can know it?" (Jeremiah 17:9).

"For I know that in me (that is, in my flesh,) dwelleth no good thing: for to will is present with me; but how to perform that which is good I find not. For the good that I would I do not: but the evil which I would not, that I do. Now if I do that I would not, it is no more I that do it, but sin that dwelleth in me. I find then a law, that, when I would do good, evil is present with me. For I delight in the law of God after the inward man: But I see another law in my members, warring against the law of my mind, and bringing me into captivity to the law of sin which is in my members. O wretched man that I am! who shall deliver me from the body of this death?" (Romans 7:18-24).

RELATIONSHIPS AND PRIVACY

*"Why not learn to enjoy the little things
- there are so many of them."*

~ Saint John Chrysostom

As adults, we all need to understand that when we are in a marriage or courtship relationship, it is between only two people and not with several people. If you let several people into your relationship, they will bring their prejudices into it. And if you take in what they say, then you will end up with their problems.

In starting a relationship, it is advisable to look for adults who have their own heads and not the heads of others. It is not fair to go out looking for a relationship when you are full with other people. In other words, you are not entirely yourself; you are many people. Emptiness of oneself is a prerequisite of a godly relationship. A godly relationship is empty of humanity and steadfast upon divinity.

Relationships involve two people, and sharing your relationships in a manner not worthy can be very destructive. You need to understand that you are not meant to get along with everybody. Thinking that people are always going to do right by you can be very destructive, and that is why it is your responsibility to protect a good relationship, if you have one. A lot of relationships are destroyed today because people are more focused on what other people are doing, and they are never focused in making sure that their home lives and relationships are healthy.

It is very unfair to ask your friends for advice about your intimacy when your mate has no clue about what is going on. It is a worldly and ungodly spirit. The same people you ask for advice about your relationship may sabotage it, then sit back and watch the drama. The relationships of some people have no privacy; they take their relationships everywhere, including the workplace.

In today's world, the workplace has become a social gathering, where people bring too much of their personal stuff. They fail to understand that work is work, and home is home. Love triangles, fornication, and adultery can occur at the workplace. People spend more time talking about their personal life on the job than their business life until they begin to crash. Some are deceived to believe that their co-workers are doing better. The reality is that a lot of people fake it, but behind closed doors, they have lots of problems. These are the same folks who will badmouth your mate, but if they have the opportunity, they will want your mate. Some get into a relationship with the suspicious idea that the other person will not be faithful. Such a thing is a result of previous baggage and mentality of self. Focus on your partner with trust and faithfulness. You are not God. Take life daily and learn to deal with whatever comes.

You may have a hard-working mate who works about seventy-five hours a week, while you are home, talking and telling your friends about what you like and want. You talk to friends on the phone and still do not get enough, and you jump into social media groups, blogs, and chat rooms, only to get more confused. You begin to receive advice, such as, "Your man is not making enough money, and you are too pretty to settle for less," or, "It is boring staying home with your children," or, "Besides, your husband is too short." You keep hearing all types of stuff that could apply to your husband. It begins to affect you, and you start feeling unhappy because you have been listening to the same devils over and over. You finally fall for all the advice you have received on the job and from friends. Their description of your happiness finally comes along. You quickly forget that you wanted a family, and you wanted to settle down. Your mate may not have done anything wrong, but you desperately want out because you think you found something better. You work very hard to find reasons to get rid of your mate or to get a divorce, and you succeed. You begin to date someone who meets the description of your friends and advisors. You boast about this person to your friends and say, "I finally got my baby. He is tall and sexy." You date for a couple years, but this person never talks about settling down. Your inner desire is still to have a family, but this person you are with now has no intentions of doing so. At that point, you decide to ask yourself, "Where is this relationship heading?"

The person you thought was your ideal mate responds by saying, "We are doing just fine. What are you worrying about? I do not have to be committed to you. As long as we are doing fine, that's all."

You have wasted several years, and you begin to regret the decisions you made. You say to yourself, "Had I known, I could have stayed with my ex. My ex was hard working and was a family person." Now, you realize that there may be good people out there, but they are difficult to find.

The key here is that we must protect the privacy of good relationships. I am not saying protect an abusive relationship. I do not support abuse of God's image in any way.

Takeaways:
Protect the privacy and intimacy of a marriage and family by understanding that there will always be some small issues.

YOU CAN BE INFLUENCED BY GAB

"For he that will love life, and see good days, let him refrain his tongue from evil, and his lips that they speak no guile: Let him eschew evil, and do good; let him seek peace, and ensue it. For the eyes of the Lord are over the righteous, and his ears are open unto their prayers: but the face of the Lord is against them that do evil."

~ 1 Peter 3:10-12

The lives of many have veered in multiple directions because of influence. Some people have the gift of gab, and by the time they are finished with you, you will believe that the sky is all red. It is a dangerous thing to fall in the hands of those with the gift of gab. Their words are so powerful and are capable of spurring the naive to actions they would usually not take. And after you are dealt with gab, you are usually left to feel stupid. If you are in the habit of listening to people with a quixotic mentality about life, then you have no one to blame when you find yourself in a deep mess.

At one point in time, most of us have found ourselves in plights that resulted from listening to others. There are ramifications as to how we respond to every situation in life. Gab can ruin lives and deceive people. "A lying tongue hateth those that are afflicted by it; and a flattering mouth worketh ruin" (Proverbs 26:28).

I am not saying that I am any better, but the weak minded can be easily manipulated. We are all subject to deception if we are not careful. It seems that people typically want to be led, and they generally gravitate to authoritative kinds of individuals. I am not against people voluntarily submitting themselves to each other or being mutually submissive for the common good. I am against forced submission.

Others tend to listen to their buddies because they think they have a bond. Knowing yourself prevents you from being influenced or acting in an irrational way. People's lives are shaped by certain belief systems or values; these are derived from various circumstances. In a capitalist society, our values are related to materialism, status, and celebrities through which or whom most of us are easily influenced.

Whether you believe it or not, the words or actions of people can change the whole direction of your life for better or for worse. Most people tend to live their lives after the lives of those they consider entertainment idols. In reality, so many have made entertainment their lifestyles. Most of what entertainers do is vile and profane.

It is very beneficial to discern those with the gift of gab. We know that some people are full of stuff that is not necessarily good. We need to be able to know when people are wrong and when we should not submit to their fallacies and ideas. Those with the gift of gab will talk to you for the purpose of getting something out of you. It is advisable to find an escape route to stop listening to them before you get carried away. Those with the gift of gab know their audience. They know what people want to hear. The Bible warns us about discernment of such folks: "For they that are such serve not our Lord Jesus Christ, but their own belly; and by good words and fair speeches deceive the hearts of the simple" (Romans 16:18).

For those of you who have made a major purchase, you know when a salesman on commission is trying to sell you something. All he thinks about is his commission, not minding the problems after the deal. After the purchase, the sales person has no business with you. You then may have to deal with creditors or collectors. Can you imagine if someone with the gift of gab comes to you and asks you for hundreds of dollars and informs you that he will double that money? What on earth will cause you to believe such a person? If they have that capability, they will be doubling their own money and not yours. Scams are so common these days, from email scams, to social media scams, to in-person scams, and religious scams. The list goes on and on.

It is good to know that most people do not have your best interest in most situations; rather, they are out for their own interests. It is too bad that you can't trust anyone these days, but it is the reality. Although it is sometimes not done on purpose, when it comes down to the wire, people tend to look out for their own interests.

You can't call them at three a.m. when you have a problem. Some will respond briefly, but if the problems persist, they will quickly disappear. Those you thought were your friends will prove themselves otherwise. That is why you only need to tell people who really need to know your business.

Most of us could have had more rewarding and productive lives if we could have believed in what God wanted for our lives and not what others want for us. Let us be mindful of those with the gift of gab who influence our desires to wane from what God wants for us. One can avoid being influenced by others by discerning their motives.

Takeaway:

"Let no man deceive you with vain words: for because of these things cometh the wrath of God upon the children of disobedience" (Ephesians 5:6).

THE WORKPLACE DISEASE

"We hate to have some people give us advice because we know how badly they need it themselves."

~ Laurence J. Peter

The workplace disease is an illness that most of us aren't aware of, but it is a serious one indeed. It has destroyed families, careers, relationships, and friendships in most cases.

People spend more time on the job than with their families. The bond that many create on the job and elsewhere is usually stronger than the bond at home in some situations. But it needs to be understood that work is not the place to bring all your problems. You do not go to work to be liked; you get to work to get paid. Employers have the right to ensure that your energy is used to benefit them.

It is not appropriate to bring your personal business to work. You are either going to get in trouble, or too many people are going to know what is going on in your personal life. If you love to tell people about every personal area in your life, you are giving people weapons to use against you.

It can be very dangerous for people with good and stable relationships to form personal emotional bonds at the workplace. This has resulted in broken marriages and relationships. Many people with good relationships have been wrongly influenced by coworkers. The moment they have some disagreement with their mates, they run to the coworkers they have a bond with. They say all sorts of negative things about their mates, running them down like water. Most times, they end up in a relationship with the same person they talk to about their problems. When this happens, they go home mad and angry with their mates. They will search for every excuse for separation or divorce. Such people never cared about their mates in the first place. They treat their spouses badly on purpose, and they can't wait to get home to tell them off. They become very unfair to their mates by not expressing their feelings or talking about their problems to them. They will tell their friends or coworkers everything, but not their mates. To them, it doesn't matter whether the other person wants to work things out or not. Their minds have been poisoned and made up by the workplace disease. They believe they have found the right and perfect person at work. It is only when they realize that the coworker was just for fun or sex that they will want to return to their mates. But sometimes, it is too late. Some are lucky to be accepted again, but others had no opportunity to do so. Yes, they were bamboozled because they do not think for themselves. The tricksters heard them talk about how bad their relationship was, and they took advantage of it. Abusers and deceivers understand how to read emotions so that they can respond appropriately to get what they want. I am not saying there are no bad relationships or abusive ones, but know the scope of the issue and address it according to the law. I do not believe in perpetual abuse or any form of abuse.

Most times, these outcomes are not surprising because such relationships start in negative situations. That is why it is usually easy for infidelity to occur.

Ignorance also plays a very important role in office romance. For example, if you are happily married and come across a co-worker who wants to be with you so badly that it doesn't matter whether you are married or not, common sense will tell you that he or she is not a good person to be around. The reason is that such a person does not respect any relationship, and you will be played. If he or she doesn't care whether you are married or not, what makes you think that they will care about you? Is this not ignorance?

In today's world, it seems as if most people go to work, not only for business, but also to find happiness and companionship that fulfills their lustful vices. Whether an organization or a corporation supports social activities or groups or not, people will form cliques. They will do so by attracting those who think they have the same interests or think the same way. Their desire is to create a social situation in the workplace. Some find happiness by going out with co-workers, partying and drinking together. Even those who have beautiful families easily find themselves falling into such traps.

Most times, people do not realize that they are making themselves look bad and stupid by not doing their job right. They spend most of their day talking or seeking romance and think that employers deserve a lackluster performance. The job is not about who you like or do not like; it is about you doing your job.

Some people want to do anything but their job. The same folks who do not want to work are the same folks who are always complaining about their jobs. They go around saying that they are not getting paid enough, so they do their work carelessly. Usually, most people with such attitudes are the ones who have been on the job for years, yet do not know the job. They have the workplace disease because they do not want to work and learn; they only want to play. They encourage others not to work hard because they are not working hard themselves. As a result, there is low productivity.

I hate working around people who are always complaining. Even if there is no problem around, they will find a problem or a way to make one. They will never talk about their own problems because it seems that everyone has a problem but them. Even though they have no idea about what is being talked about, they will quickly jump into any conversation when they hear them talking about something. Some come to work boasting about their vacations, families, and even their social life.

They will do so even when they are not asked. Their private lives are put in the open. They will spend most of their time on the job talking when work needs to be done.

On the whole, we need to remember who we were at the interview before we got the job. After we got that job, we met new people and got into their cliques, and they made us a different person. It's possible that we used to be happy going home from work, but all that changed. Now, we might go home mad, angry, and confused. All our social energy could be spent at work, and now, we may have nothing left for home. We find excuses to dump or leave our mates for something we thought was better on the job. This is how ignorantly most allow the workplace to make them a different person.

Takeaway:
Don't let the job make you a different person.

DECISION TIME

> *"You have enemies? Good. That means you have stood up for something, sometime in your life."*
>
> ~ *Winston Churchill*

The public can't make personal decisions for us. We will only be confused and undecided all the time if we depend on public opinions to make sound decisions with less risks and liabilities. Public opinion is not full of wisdom. If we do not make a decision about our lives, situations and events will make the decision for us, so there is no escape.

Decisions about what we want in life should be made of our own volition and are not to be influenced by anyone. It is never a problem if what God wants for us is what we want. The fear of God is the beginning of good decisions (Proverbs 14:2). Wise decisions lead to success, and bad decisions lead to so many headaches and drama. Most decisions we make in life do have long-term effects that can be either beneficial or destructive. So do not take making decisions carelessly. Running first to God opens

107

our eyes to see things as God sees them and not how we see them from our self perspective. Self perspective can be deceiving and damaging in the long run, and it can lead to selfish and destructive decisions. Self is corrupt and defiled (Proverbs 3:5-6).

In Matthew 5:33-37, we can use the emphasis Jesus placed on oath keeping and apply that to our decision-making process. We must decide on what God wants for us and settle with it. The answer is either "yes" or "no," not "maybe" or "sometimes." We should decide on a life that God has given us and move forward with it because a "double-minded man is unstable in all his ways" (James 1:8). Being unstable in decisions affects our personal business, family, social, and spiritual lives. It is impossible to travel on opposite lanes at the same time. We have got to pick the lanes that lead to our destinations and stay on them. Trying to be in several lanes at the same time to reach several destinations is confusing.

God will not only help you decide, but He will also show you the path of your decision and help you along the way. This alone should encourage and motivate you to come out of self will and depend on God's will at the cross (Psalm 32:8).

If we get out of ourselves and trusting only in God for good decisions, we will clearly follow the right path that leads to good and moral decisions. The right people in our lives will help guide us to the right choices (Proverbs 15:22). Interacting with wise people also assists us in decision making (Proverbs 13:20).

Associating with those who only support your views will lead to bad choices. They will not tell you whether you are right or wrong. Corrupt and vile friends will corrupt your decision-making process. However, a mature person will not ignore advice. He will assess and look at everything before he comes to a conclusion. On the other hand, the fool has his mind made up. He will listen to no one. He goes by the feelings of his natural senses derived from sinful nature. He will not see as God sees, so he will fall into destruction. We can no longer afford to continue life with destructive circumstances, people, and behaviors accompanying us. We cannot be obtuse, acting as if we are ignorant of people, issues, and behaviors that keep misery in our lives. It is our responsibility to decide who or what stays or leaves our lives. A confused person usually has sundry decisions about one particular issue. Most of us may know the precariousness of associating with certain folks, but we do so anyway.

The daily decisions we make will change the course of our lives. Decisions are not to be taken carelessly. Letting other people decide for us will alter the course of our lives, too. It is always a good idea to scrutinize available options before making a major decision. I don't necessarily fault people who are still finding their way. If you are afraid to fail or try, you will never be able to take the steps needed to move you to the next level. Lots and lots of people are still trying to find their way because we were all lost at one time. We can find grace in Christ.

Certain people need to be allowed to experience the up and downs of reality by deciding for themselves due to their stubbornness and made-up minds. There is nothing we can do if people avoid useful information before making a decision. They are not going to have the same group of folks around them all the time.

You are responsible for deciding your life after God's counsel. Those around you will not have to answer for any decision you make. Many people are in sad situations today because they let others choose and answer for them. This has led to broken families, broken relationships, and broken careers. Decisions based solely on emotions and natural affections may not be best. Good decisions are based on moral truth, and moral truths have been time tested. They may not be popular, but they are life.

Takeaways:

You are responsible to listen and look at the wisdom of God's Word before making decisions.

Choose divine wisdom, and you will not fall to the trap of self.

THE SERENITY OF STAYING OUT OF WHAT IS NOT YOUR BUSINESS

God, grant me the serenity to accept the things I cannot change, the courage to change the things I can, and the wisdom to know the difference.

~ Reinhold Niebuhr, "The Serenity Prayer"

Many are restless and troubled because they try to stay in what is not their business. Just imagine the effort people put in things that do not concern them and are not beneficial to family and community. It can be very challenging to live a life of serenity if we have too many activities going on in our lives. Our lives become so complicated when we focus on little things that just do not matter. We need to start getting back to the basics of life. Our lives could be much improved if we spend optimum time to make it better by staying within our

God-ordained boundaries and business. Taking control of our lives with God's help through Christ cannot be procrastinated; it needs to be done now. Peace and stability of mind is not necessarily the absence of a perfect environment, but it is instead calmness in a situation of chaos. We can be calm by not allowing people or events to control our spirits and souls.

One way to stay calm in life is developing the tranquility of a state of mind, which can only be achieved by having the mind of Christ. The mind of Christ is a mind stayed on the Lord, and the work of the Holy Spirit delivers peace to our minds. A mind stayed on the lord receives constant delivery of peace in the midst of a world in trouble or commotion. "Thou wilt keep him in perfect peace, whose mind is stayed on thee: because he trusteth in thee" (Isaiah 26:3). This is a peace that activity cannot achieve. It is a peace that the world's richest could not achieve. It is a peace that the mighty and powerful could not achieve. This peace is contingent upon a mind staying on the Lord. This peace is given by Christ Jesus as our minds are stayed on the Lord: "Peace I leave with you; my peace I give you. I do not give to you as the world gives. Do not let your hearts be troubled and do

not be afraid" (John 14:27 NIV). The guarantee of peace
in an environment where everything seems to be falling
apart begins when we stay out of what is not our
business and start focusing on the peace God gives.
Trying to involve oneself in unnecessary arguments and
debates never guarantees peace. God provides peace that
we can't understand because the peace He provides is
not based on what we have or do not have, nor is it based
on our condition.

Let us learn to accept the things we can't control. This
does not mean that we should accept anything that
comes our way because everything that comes our way is
not what God wants for us. But common sense should
tell us that we can't control other people's actions or
choices, and as a result, their actions should not be taken
personally. We can't control what people think or do. We
also need to understand that we don't own the world,
and we can't even manage the world for a second, so why
worry?

Trying to gain the entire world is also an issue. It drains
us, and we get nothing out of it. This is something we
should remember and practice regularly. When it comes

to past events, they are gone. We can't bring them back. We can't be living a life that focuses on our regrets and failures. We can't leave the past in our minds if we want to leave it behind us. Going back will steal our peace. My advice is for us to leave and avoid what we can't change when we realize the matter. Rushing and trying to force our way on things that we can change will lead to more unrest, anger, and immorality. We need to slow down and stop being anxious as best we can.

Some areas in this modern era that steal value from our lives and subtract from our days are the media and, in turn, the internet. The media is an outside force that can seize or trouble your eternal life. In other words, the media wants to capture your life by capturing your soul. We should also learn to understand that everything on the internet does not pertain to us. Everything is not our business. With the exception of business-related matters, things like notifications can be turned off and checked later. We can't respond to everyone and everything we hear or see.

Dr. Phil McGraw, in an NBC news interview, noted the distractions and issues from the internet that can bring unrest in our lives if not regulated: "The Internet is just bringing all kinds of information into the home. There's just a lot of distraction, a lot of competition for the parent's voice to resonate in the children's ears" (McGraw.) Our minds were never meant to be slaves of the media, wandering from place to place. The abundance of information can be very destructive if we allow it to blitz our minds. We must control our intake of the media. The media should not be controlling our souls. It is very dangerous to get to the point where we are incited to both offend people and be offended. This should be avoided because it drains so much life out of us.

One way to have peace and calmness is through love. One will never have peace without the love of God. We are commanded to love our neighbors as we love ourselves (Mark 12:31) and to follow peace with everyone. People full of hate are not peaceful people, for they are always troubled by their hate.

Living from within leads to great peace because the spirit of God within us is greater than any situation externally. "Ye are of God, little children, and have overcome them:

because greater is he that is in you, than he that is in the world" (1 John 4:4). Let us learn to live daily as overcomers and not drown by focusing too much on tomorrow. Tomorrow will take care of itself. We are only responsible for today. We should never get to the point of becoming children of the media.

It is not necessary and profitable to surround ourselves by people and things that force us to accept the life they provide. There is much peace in spending the little time we have in life by focusing on those things that are necessary and needful for life. Let us focus on things that give life.

Takeaways:

No human being has had it all, done it all, and been it all.

Do not be deceived; we all have an appointment with death.

HOW DO YOU KEEP YOURSELF OUT OF WHAT IS NOT YOUR BUSINESS?

"And that ye study to be quiet, and to do your own business, and to work with your own hands, as we commanded you."

~ 1 Thessalonians 4:11

Suffering from agitation as a result of unwarranted interference in other people's business is a self-inflicted pain. We must do our best to heal from this self-inflicted disease. This may not be easy for so many who have, for a long time, practiced the habit of intruding in things that do not concern them.

The best way to keep yourself out of what is not your business is to focus on what is your business. Being idle and focusing on what has nothing to do with improving your family and the lives of others is useless and hopeless. So many are troubled and unproductive today because their focus is not on their life's mission. They are focused on what everyone else is doing as they neglect the uniqueness within them by trying to be involved with everything and include everyone on their ship.

If we discipline ourselves to focus on our God-given missions, we will have little or no time in trying to be involved in everything that does not pertain to us. Living a mission-focused life saves us a lot of headache. We are not God, and we need to stop worrying about what is going to happen or what others are going to do.

To keep ourselves out of others' business, we must be determined to lead a quiet life. Peace comes when we understand that God is sovereign and not us. This is why we need to rest in Christ to cease from doing what only a sovereign God can do. We need to stay out of what we can't be because we can't be all things on earth; what we can't do because we can't do everything on earth, and what we can't have because we can't have everything on earth.

Let us not confuse this with what scripture says that we can do all things through Christ who strengthens us (Philippians 4:13). God will not allow us to do all things when all things we do are not His will. This is talking about divine power and not self power. The point here is keeping yourself out of what is not your business or your calling. Staying out of what is not your business will allow you to focus more on becoming excellent in what is your business. Staying out of what is not your business will save you more time and resources to invest on your life's mission. "Seest thou a man diligent in his business? he shall stand before kings; he shall not stand before mean men" (Proverbs 22:29). Your craft will not be perfected if you are always spending time on what is not your business. We should all spend time in developing and perfecting whatever craft God has given us.

In staying out of what is not our business, we are commanded to study to be quiet, meaning it requires effort, wisdom, and understanding to leave certain things alone. In other words, if we can't stay quiet, we can't focus on anything. We need to know our limits in all things. We are also commanded to focus on what God has called us to do so that we can become independent of others and society. We can become an example and not a liability to so many in society by exercising freedom to focus and work on our natural talents. By wasting the time on our hands on other peoples' business, we become dormant to our own business. Time on our hands should be used to work on what we need to do and not for meddling in everything that does not pertain to us. Idle people who are involved in everything that's not their business are usually not focused on anything.

The world will only benefit from us when we stay out of people's business and focus on our service to the world by perfecting our uniqueness. There are so many little things we can do daily to keep ourselves out of what is not our business. I have made some suggestions below. There is more to say about keeping yourself out of other people's business, and there is more to say about keeping ourselves out of things that do not pertain to us. But I hope the following suggestions will help.

1) Understand that people and events are not the measuring standard for your life.
2) Don't let the events of this world and the way other people see life affect you.
3) Plan your day and take inventory at the end of each day to see how much time was wasted on what is not your business. Make corrections the next day.

4) Acknowledge God in all your ways by submitting what you want to do for Him for approval through prayer and consecration.

5) Understand the preciousness of time on your hands. If you waste it, you can't get it back. Redeem the time you have wasted on meddling.

6) Avoid the baits of being dragged into things that steal life from you.

7) Turn off notifications and log off social sites that do not pertain to work or business. Schedule social media. Learning to log off social media is a good thing.

8) Learn to stay away from people you don't know when they start getting personal. Avoid the conversation when you know that it is getting personal.

9) Set alarms on various times of the day to remind yourself of how your time is being spent. Do this until you mature in becoming conscious of your time.

10) Ensure that your task at hand is completed before you check social media; otherwise,

you may forget about your task. Block out social media activities if you have uncompleted tasks. Your task is your business.

11) Do not trust outside your circle of trust; they must be people of the cross. It is sad to say, but you should not trust anyone. A lifetime partner or, sometimes, close relatives or siblings can be an exception to this rule, but it is up to you. The exception is noted because these are the folks who really care sometimes. They are the folks who will put money together to bail you out when you are in trouble. It is sometimes good to keep certain things to yourself or between you and God.

12) Limit your communication and communicate openly when you do. It is good to be able to talk to everyone and openly. Talking openly reduces the ability of the communication from becoming too personal.

13) Learn to recognize liars and know how to deal with them.

14) Understand that people will use your own words against you. They will repeat what you say.

15) Be wise with unstable people and situations.

16) Avoid going for counseling to people you know. These folks are not professionals. They have no confidentiality agreement, and they will put your business out there without even knowing it. The exception is up to you.

17) It is a very big mistake to ask the whole world for counseling or advice. Some people just have too many friends, and almost every friend is a confidant. It is best to seek an expert's advice before you decide on serious issues.

18) Stay away from those who want to make you their remote control. Treat control freaks with a spoon and a long arm. It is not always easy to identify control freaks. This is because they come into your life as well-meaning people. They may be people who have contributed greatly to your life.

19) Ignore the ignorance and move on, and in some circumstances, your best bet is to do so. Everyone is not going to understand what you have been through. They will not understand your pain and agony. They have no idea of your secret place nor the skeletons in your closet. They see and judge you at face value. The point is that you will have no peace if you try to make everyone understand. As long as you are not exactly what people want you to be, they will not understand you.

20) Protect yourself and your family from being used as a public property. Protecting yourself and your family is all about serenity. It is your responsibility to protect your family from gossip, slander, back biting, control, and any forms or destructive influence. You have no control over what people say. Don't let it settle in your head. Be wise.

21) You do not need friends who think that you are less than nothing. Why waste time with those who contribute absolutely nothing to

your life? It can be very painful to force yourself on those who keep rejecting you. I understand that some people desire to be connected to certain people. Let the choosing be yours. If they come, show them love, but learn to know when to leave people alone.

22) There are two sides to every story. Learn to listen before you get yourself involved or take sides. I suggest not taking sides at all as a Christian. Follow Biblical truth.

23) Do not tolerate gossip mongers and rumor mongers.

24) Your destruction begins when you start surrounding yourself with gossip and rumor mongers. It is very unhealthy to be around people with these crazy attributes.

25) You can talk to people and tell them absolutely nothing about yourself. Learn to use wisdom.

26) Learn to understand that you are competing with yourself and not with anyone else.

27) Obey the law of the land, as long as it does not go against what God wants personally for you.

28) Value what God wants for you more than what you want for yourself. What God wants for you is found in His Word.

Takeaways:

Understand the preciousness of the time on your hands daily.

Take inventory of how you use your time daily.

Time wasted will not come back to you.

WORKS CITED

McGraw, Phil, et al. "Transcript for Dec. 26." *NBCNews.com*, NBC Universal News Group, 26 Dec. 2004, www.nbcnews.com/id/wbna6755915.

All beginning-of-chapter quotes attributed to their respective authors.

ABOUT THE AUTHOR

It is not about the author, but about the cross of Jesus Christ. Therefore, this excerpt is only for informational purposes for the curious.

The author desires readers to view him as one who was once bound and controlled by the prince and power of the air and walked according to the course of this world, the spirit that now worketh in the children of disobedience (Ephesians 2:2). He was unfit and unworthy to take the cross and undeserving of grace, but the grace of God, which carries salvation to all, still appeared to him through a God who so dearly loves him and gave His only Son for him (John 3:16). His unworthiness of the grace which has been so freely poured on him makes him see himself as the least among the saints to whom this grace was given to preach the unsearchable riches of Christ (Ephesians 3:8). His greatest accomplishment is the acceptance of this unmerited grace through repentance.

The author lives in western Maryland with his family and is a citizen of God's kingdom. His current spiritual address within the body of Christ is Virginia Avenue Church of God, where he leads the prayer ministry.

John Genda's main focus areas of ministries are:

- **HOPAC (Household of Parents and Children)** - Helps parents and children understand their God-given responsibilities to each other and how to perform them in a balanced and healthy manner.

- **POG (Presence of God)** - The desperation of the early church to pursue the life of God as recorded in Acts Chapter two, resulting in true fellowship with one another and with God, transmitted life to a dead world.

- **BEAM (Backyard Evangelism and Missions)** - BEAM helps churches to reach out to as many people as possible within the one-mile radius of their location intentionally and regularly.

Although the author is ordained and holds degrees in Biblical Studies, Paralegal Studies, Cybersecurity, and multiple certifications, he has no glory in such accomplishments. He counts all things as dung for the sake of the humble cross of Christ, not to be boastful of any status (Philippians 3:8).

The author prays not to be in the sad, empty state of placing much emphasis on things of vanity as human status and accomplishments, as stated by the preacher: "Vanity of vanities, saith the Preacher, vanity of vanities; all is vanity" (Ecclesiastes 1:2). He is humbled to continually pursue the cross.

He is the organizer of CLEAN PAGE fellowship, an association of individuals who believe in pursuing what God wants and encouraging others to do likewise. Also, he offers free cross life leadership training for startup churches and young people free of charge.

Please visit www.johngenda.org for further information.

www.ingramcontent.com/pod-product-compliance
Lightning Source LLC
Chambersburg PA
CBHW060311050426
42448CB00009B/1788